Pino the Pigeon

Pino the Pigeon

Catherine Burigo

First paperback edition 2023

Book design by Publishingpush

978-1-80541-136-9 (paperback)
978-1-80541-138-3 (hardback)
978-1-80541-137-6 (ebook)

For Emilia, Leo and Phoebe,

Remember – work hard,

be kind, have fun, eat lunch.

All my love xxx

Pino woke up in his old oak tree.
Alone in his nest he felt melancholy.
He yawned, he stretched, he got out of bed
and up popped the feathers on top of his head.

This huge tuft of feathers made Pino feel sad.
It made him look different and different was bad.
He wanted to be the same as the rest.
Same was better. Same was best.

Worm poked out from his hole in the ground.

With an air of arrogance Worm looked around.

He was the Boss and laid down the law.

Worm was a bully and hard to ignore.

"Hey Punk," Worm shouted, *"with that tuft on your head.*

When will you listen to what I've said?

You don't belong here. Take yourself off.

It's best for everyone if you just get lost."

Worm's gang joined in. *"Yeah, Pino,"* they said,

"with that tuft of white feathers on top of your head.

You look like a skunk and smell like one too.

Come on Pino, you know what to do."

Pino swallowed his tears and climbed back in his nest.

The worms were right. Leaving was best.

He wasn't wanted. He couldn't stay.

First thing tomorrow, he'd run away.

Pino knew of a place, Trafalgar Square.
A pigeon-uncle of his lived there.
It was *full* of pigeons his uncle had said,
maybe one who might have a tuft on *their* head.

The morning arrived and Pino was ready.
He climbed down his tree, slow and steady.
No sign of Worm, Pino started to run.
When Worm woke up, Pino was gone.

KITTY

Across the road, Pino spied Cat

who was having a drink of milk on her mat.

"Hello, Cat," called Pino. *"I say, you, over there!*

Do you know the way to Trafalgar Square?"

"Ha ha!" laughed Cat. *"Look at your head!*

If I were you, I'd hide in bed.

Trafalgar Square? Well now, let me see.

How can I help you most helpfully?"

She licked her lips and sharpened her claws
and lunged for Pino with her feline jaws.
A bus pulled up and the doors opened wide.
Pino saw his chance and jumped inside.

He ran to the back and slid under the seat,
right next to Dog who was chewing a treat.
"Hello, Dog," said Pino. *"I say, you, under there!*
Do you know the way to Trafalgar Square?"

"GRRR," growled Dog, guarding his bone.

"Get lost, pigeon, leave me alone.

And by the way, you've got fluff on your head.

You should be a chicken instead."

"Get that bird off my bus!" the driver shouted,

jumping up and looking excited.

A woman screamed. A child started to cry.

Pino crept backwards, trying to hide.

The driver grabbed Pino and squeezed him tight.
Pino gulped, wide-eyed with fright.
He pecked the driver hard on his thumb,
slipped from his grip and made for a run.

Pino jumped right off the bus,
immediately tangled in the morning tube rush.
Shoes and umbrellas, bags and boots,
unsmiling people in stiff black suits.

public UNDERGROUND Subway

He tumbled and rolled down hard concrete steps.
Down, down, down, into London's dark depths.
Never so far had a poor pigeon tumbled,
until onto the tube tracks, he finally stumbled.

Rubbing his head, he looked around.
He could hear the most bewildering sound.
A roaring monster with yellow eyes
of a terrifyingly enormous size
was speeding towards him out of the dark,
screeching and steaming and shooting off sparks.

Pino froze on the spot, so great was his fear.

"That's it," he thought. *"It all ends here."*

The monster got closer. No way out.

Then from the tunnel there came a shout.

"Lie flat," said the voice. It was squeaky and high.

"Then the train will pass you by."

"Look, like this," the squeaky voice said

pushing Pino down on his head.

"Ouch" said Pino. *"What are you doing?"*

"I'm saving your life. You've got to get moving."

As the train passed over, Pino squeezed his eyes shut.

"Well now," said Rat, *"that was a spot of good luck! So, how did you get here? And you're going to...where? And by the way, you've got* ***magnificent*** *hair."*

"I do?" said Pino, blushing a little.
The compliment made his tummy tickle.
"Well, actually, I'm going to Trafalgar Square. I'm going to find a real friend there."

"I can take you," said Rat. *"I know the way.*

Navigating the underground for me is child's play.

We can run through the tunnels if you don't mind the dark.

I can get us back up at St James's Park.

A quick hop through the grass and we'll be there.

Pigeon heaven; Trafalgar Square!"

They crawled through the tunnels, Rat taking the lead,

crouching down when a train came at high speed.

It really was the most terrifying thing

but Rat was careful to look after him.

"That's it. We're here," Rat eventually said.

It's time to go up and poke out our heads!"

Up, up, up the grey concrete stairs.

Up, up, up to Trafalgar Square.

"Hmm, I'm confused," said Rat, scratching her ear.

"This building didn't used to be here.

That statue didn't used to be there.

It all looks different. I wonder why?

The Square has moved, Pino!" and she let out a sigh.

"Oh Rat," wailed Pino. *"You said you could do it!"*

"And I will!" said Rat. *"Have faith. Stick to it!"*

Then a dad and a mum with two little boys
bustled past making lots of noise.
"We're tired," moaned the boys. *"We can't walk anymore."*
And they promptly threw themselves on the floor!

"I know what we need," said the weary dad.

"We need to find a taxi cab."

He put out his arm and a taxi pulled over.

He leant through the window and spoke to the driver.

"Trafalgar Square, please," said the dad.

"Pino!" exclaimed Rat. "*Follow that cab!*"

Pino began to flap his wings
and what happened next was an amazing thing.
His red, scaly feet took off from the floor
and he flew like he never had before!

Rat jumped on his back and held on to his tuft
and the two of them flew up and up.
"Oh, Rat," cried Pino, *"what a beautiful sky.
I've been so afraid, I forgot I could fly!"*
"Woo, hoo!" shouted Rat, punching the air.
*"Onwards, to Trafalgar Square!
Your tuft is so perfect for steering us there.
I'd slide off your back with no handle of hair."*

They followed the taxi and soon they were there,
soaring over the impressive Square.
Nelson's Column, tall and proud,
fountains and lions and tourists in crowds.

Most impressive, there were pigeons galore.
Pino couldn't have imagined more.
Black, white and grey, short, tall and thin.
Whatever you looked like, you'd be sure to fit in.
Orange beaks, yellow beaks, pink legs and more.
Here, being different wasn't a flaw.

They rested a while and took in the view.

Deep in his heart, Pino knew what to do.

"I want to go home, Rat," Pino said.

Rat looked perplexed and shook her head.

"We've only just got here. Why should we go?

Look for a friend, you'll find one I know."

"I've already found her," Pino smiled.

"She's small and feisty and a little bit wild.

She's got pointy, grey teeth and red, beady eyes

and a big personality, considering her size."

“She sounds awesome,” said Rat, *“good work, young man.*

Everything has gone according to plan.

I’ll step aside and let you get on.

It’s been good to meet you. So long! So long!”

Rat hung her head and tiptoed away.

Secretly, she wanted to stay.

*“Hey, Rat, come back! It’s **you**, silly thing!*

Because of you I found my wings!

***You’re** my friend. The best one ever.*

I feel brave and happy when we’re together!”

"But I want to go back, Rat, back to my tree.
I won't let Worm and his gang bother me.
Will you come? Say you will. I won't do it alone.
Will you help me, Rat, to get back home?"
"Why, of course!" cried Rat, punching the air.
"With me beside you, Worm won't dare!"

Pino flapped his wings and began to take off.
Rat jumped on his back and held on to his tuft.
"Woo, hoo!" said Rat, punching the sky.
"Look at my friend! He can fly! He can fly!"
They flew all the way back to Pino's tree,
brave and excited, happy and free.

Worm poked out from his hole in the ground.

"Hey Punk," **shouted Worm,** *"you're back I see.*

Back to hide in your lonely tree.

You've still got that ridiculous tuft on your head.

Let's just call you Skunk instead."

Pino wasn't scared of Worm anymore.

"What's it like down there, Worm, stuck on the floor?

"I'm not a punk or a skunk. I'm a pigeon with flare.

I'm proud of my tuft of white fluffy hair.

I won't hide away. I've got too much to do.

And the first thing I'm doing is ignoring you!"

Worm looked shocked and slid back in the ground,
no match for the bravery Pino had found.
So, Pino and Rat became the firmest of friends
and that is how this story ends.

Same is not better. Same is not best.
You don't need to be like all the rest.
Wear your tuft like a crown.
Spread your wings and fly high.
Be like Pino and reach for the sky.